Monkey Business

Mr Jolly was a zoo keeper. One sunny mornin
jumped out of bed and into his slipper
gown. 'It's a wonderful day,' he th
best way to start a wonderful day i
breakfast. Now what's my favourite

Mr Jolly had a problem. All food was his favourite food. He went to the stove and began to cook. Before long, the most delicious smells were coming from Mr Jolly's kitchen. They were the sort of smells you would like to wake up to. Thick, tasty sausages sizzled under the grill. Six slices of bacon fizzed and sputtered. There were eggs, tomatoes and mushrooms. Mr Jolly sang to himself as he buttered his toast and slurped his coffee. I regret to say that Mr Jolly's table manners were not as good as yours or mine.

When Mr Jolly had finished his breakfast he washed and dressed for work, and went out to feed the animals in the zoo.

He gave the seals their fish.

He gave the elephants their hay.

And he gave the tigers ten tins of cat food, each.

Last of all, Mr Jolly went to feed Chuckles the chimpanzee. He was Mr Jolly's favourite. Mr Jolly spent a lot of time telling jokes to Chuckles. 'Morning,' he said. 'What do you get if you cross a kangaroo with a sheep?' Chuckles shook his head. 'Woolly jumpers!' laughed Mr Jolly. Chuckles looked as if he'd heard this joke many times before but Mr Jolly laughed so much that the chimpanzee began to join in. Perhaps he wasn't laughing at the joke at all. Perhaps he was laughing at Mr Jolly.

Mr Jolly filled Chuckles' bowl with nuts and pieces of banana. 'Here we are,' he said. 'Here's your nice breakfast.' But when he looked at the hard dry nuts and the pieces of banana, turning brown, he began to think. 'Oh dear! Oh dear! this won't do. Did I say "nice breakfast"? It doesn't look very nice to me. I wouldn't eat it.'

He began to think of his own breakfast. 'It's not fair,' he thought. 'All Chuckles ever gets is nuts and bananas. Breakfast, dinner and tea – just nuts and bananas. And what does he get for his Sunday lunch? Nuts and bananas.'

Mr Jolly went home to make himself a cup of tea. He was thinking very hard, and muttering to himself: 'Nuts and bananas, nuts and bananas ...'

On Sunday, Mr Jolly made himself a delicious lunch. He cooked roast lamb, with lashings of mint sauce, crunchy roast potatoes with gravy, and the finest vegetables; green bendy beans and hot popping peas. But before Mr Jolly sat down to eat his lunch he took a big plate from the cupboard and piled it high with all the good things he had cooked. Then he put it on a tray and took it to Chuckles.

‘What’s black and white and dangerous and lives in a tree, Chuckles?’ he asked. ‘Don’t you know? A magpie with a catapult!’ Mr Jolly laughed so much that Chuckles began to laugh too.

‘I’ve got a special treat for you today,’ said Mr Jolly. ‘No more nuts and bananas. Today we have my own favourite Sunday lunch. Roast lamb and mint sauce!’

Chuckles stopped laughing. He sniffed at the roast lamb and pushed the plate away. ‘What ever is the matter, Chuckles?’ asked Mr Jolly. ‘Don’t you like your dinner?’

Chuckles went to the back of the cage and stuck out his bottom lip.

Mr Jolly went and sat on a bench. 'Oh dear!' he thought, 'What can I have done? I thought Chuckles would be really pleased. I've never met anybody who didn't like lamb and mint sauce.'

Then he had another idea. There was a group of schoolchildren, with their teacher, watching the seals. 'Excuse me children,' he said, 'but would you mind telling me what your favourite food is?' Some of the children voted for fishfingers, peas and chips with tomato sauce, and others voted for beefburgers, peas and chips with tomato sauce.

Mr Jolly went back to his kitchen. He cooked peas and chips with tomato sauce. He couldn't make up his mind between beefburgers and fishfingers, so he cooked them both. 'I'm sure Chuckles will like this,' he thought. 'It's a meal fit for the Queen.'

He carried the piping hot food out to Chuckles' cage. 'Hello,' said Mr Jolly. 'What's black and white and red all over? A sunburnt penguin!'
Mr Jolly laughed and laughed. Chuckles gave him a funny look. He looked as if he had nothing to laugh about. He sniffed at the plate of food and pushed it away.

'I don't know,' said Mr Jolly. 'How can I find out what Chuckles' favourite food is when he can't tell me himself.' He sat down on the bench near Chuckles' cage. There was a little boy sitting on the bench with his parents. He was eating an ice-cream.

'That's it! That's it!' shouted Mr Jolly. 'That's what Chuckles will like! Ice-cream. Everybody likes ice-cream, and I bet it's Chuckles' favourite food too.' He ran and bought Chuckles an ice-cream and took it to his cage. The little boy followed him.

'You're not going to give that chimp an ice-cream, are you?' asked the little boy.

'Well, yes I was,' said Mr Jolly. 'I want to give him a treat. I want to find out what his favourite food is.'

'Everybody knows what a chimp's favourite food is,' said the boy.

'Do they?' gasped Mr Jolly. 'Do *you* know?'

'Yes,' said the boy. 'Nuts and bananas!'

Mr Jolly knew that he had been very silly. He rushed to his house and brought Chuckles a big bowl of nuts and bananas. 'I've got a joke for you, Chuckles,' he said. 'I've just made it up. What happened when the nutty zoo keeper gave the chimp the wrong food? The chimp went bananas!'

Mr Jolly laughed and laughed. And so did Chuckles.

A Chimp for a Day

Simon was at the zoo with his Mum and Dad. He'd looked at all the animals but his favourite was Charlie the chimpanzee. He stood in front of Charlie's cage and watched him very carefully. He began to copy the things that Charlie did. He tried walking like Charlie. Then he tried to copy the noises that Charlie made.

'Whatever are you doing, Simon?' asked his Mum. Simon didn't reply. He just made chimpanzee noises.

'Ooh, ooh, eee, eee, wah, wah!'

'That's enough of that,' said Mum. 'It's time to go home.'

'Let's go back to the car,' said Dad.

Simon followed his parents to the car park. He walked like a chimp, with his arms swinging, and kept on making his chimpanzee noises.

'Get in, Simon,' said Dad, opening the back door. Simon got into the car. Then he jumped up and down on the back seat. 'Ooo, ooh, eee, eee, wah, wah!'

'Stop being a chimp and start putting your seat belt on,' said Mum.

When they got home, Simon jumped straight out of the car and climbed his favourite tree. He swung on the low branches and made his chimp noises.

'I think he really has turned into a chimpanzee,' said Dad.

'Do you think anyone will notice the difference?' said Mum.

'No. I don't,' said Dad.

Mum and Dad went indoors. Simon stayed up the tree. Mrs Perry, the next door neighbour, came out of her house. She saw Simon in the tree. 'Hello, Simon,' she called. 'What are you doing up there?'

'Ooh, ooh, eee, eee, wah, wah!' said Simon.

'Oh, I see,' said Mrs Perry. 'You're not Simon. You're a chimpanzee? Is that it?'

'Ooh, ooh, eee, eee, wah, wah!' said Simon.

'I was just going to the shops to get myself an ice-cream,' said Mrs Perry. 'I'd bring you one too, but as you're a chimp, you won't want one.'

Simon began to feel hungry. He came down from the tree and went indoors. Mum was cooking sausages, beans and mash, Simon's favourite.

'Are you still a chimp?' asked Mum.

'Ooh, ooh, eee, eee, wah, wah!' said Simon. He jumped on his chair and began to bounce up and down.

'Even chimps have to wash their hands before they eat,' said Mum. Simon pulled a funny face, but he bounced upstairs to the bathroom to wash his hands.

When he came back Mum and Dad were sitting down eating their tea. Simon jumped onto his chair.
'Ooh, ooh, eee, eee, wah, wah!' he said. There was nothing on his plate.

'These sausages are delicious,' said Dad.

'Yes they are,' said Mum. 'Do you think our chimp is hungry yet?'

'Shouldn't think so,' said Dad.

'Ooh, ooh, eee, eee, wah, wah!' wailed Simon.

Dad didn't say anything. He got up and fetched Simon's food.

'What's this?' groaned Simon.

'Chimp food,' said Mum. 'Nuts and bananas.'

Chimpanzees

Chimpanzees live in Africa in forests and grasslands. They behave very like human beings. You can tell a great deal about how a chimp is feeling by looking at its face. Just like a human being it may look happy, or sad, or frightened.
Next to humans, chimps are the most intelligent members of the ape family. They can use simple tools such as sticks and stones, and can be taught to operate simple machines.

Chimps live in groups of fifty or more. They eat mainly nuts, berries, fruit and leaves. They will also eat eggs, insects and small animals such as birds. A chimpanzee's day is spent on the ground but at night the group will sleep safely in the low branches of trees.

Chimpanzees are also good at using their voices. If one of them sees an enemy such as a snake or a leopard, he will make a loud barking noise. The rest of the group will then come to help by throwing sticks and stones at the enemy from a safe distance.

Monkeys

Chimpanzees are often called monkeys. But they are not. Monkeys have tails. Apes, such as chimpanzees, gorillas, human beings, and gibbons, do not.
Most monkeys live in countries with warm climates such as Africa, South America and Asia. Some monkeys live in very cold lands.

The noisiest monkey is the Howler Monkey. It makes a noise like a lion which can be heard as much as five kilometres away.

▲

▼

The most acrobatic monkey is the Spider Monkey. It leaps through the top branches of trees by using the tip of its long tail as an extra hand.

The Proboscis Monkey is perhaps the strangest looking. Proboscis means 'nose', and you can see from the picture why it got its name. Its huge nose swells and grows red when the animal is angry or excited.

▲

▼ ▼

The biggest and fiercest monkeys are baboons and mandrills. The mandrill looks like a baboon but has a brightly coloured face.

Leave it Until Tomorrow

The people who live in the great Brazilian forests tell this story about the little monkeys that live in the tall trees.

Every night when the sun goes down the little monkeys huddle among the branches of the Janari trees. The rain makes them cold and miserable. The wind ruffles their fur. The monkeys grumble and chatter. 'This is no good,' they say to each other. 'Tomorrow we will build ourselves houses to keep us warm and dry.'

In the morning the sun comes up. The wind drops and the rain stops. The little monkeys wake up, yawn, and stretch themselves. 'What a beautiful day!' they say. They race through the trees, chattering and laughing. All they want to do is play.

Sometimes one of the monkeys might say, ‘I thought we were going to build houses today, to keep us warm and dry through the long nights.’

‘Oh, it’s too nice a day to bother about work. We’ll build the houses tomorrow,’ say the others.

Then night falls. The sun drops and the fun stops. The little monkeys grow cold and miserable.

‘Tomorrow we really will build ourselves houses,’ they promise. But of course they never do.

The Indians of the forests have a saying. Whenever there is work to be done and someone says, ‘Oh, leave it until tomorrow!’ the others reply, ‘That’s what the little monkeys say.’

The Monkey and the Shark

There was once a cocoa tree growing by the sea. It was the favourite tree of a colobus monkey. The monkey used to bask in the hot sunshine, munching the fruit when he was hungry. Sometimes, when the monkey grew bored, he would throw cocoa fruits at the sharks that swam in the shallow water near the foot of the tree.

One day, one of the sharks spoke to the monkey. 'Throw down some fruit, little monkey,' he said. 'I'm very hungry, and I'm tired of eating fish.'

'I didn't know sharks liked cocoa,' replied the monkey.

'Oh, yes,' said the shark. 'Cocoa is my favourite food. How kind you are to be throwing it at me . . . I mean to me.'

The monkey had a kind heart. He didn't mind feeding the shark. It was fun throwing the juicy fruits into the sea and watching the great fish snap them up.

In time the monkey and the shark became great friends. 'I wish there was something I could do to repay your kindness,' said the shark. 'Would you like to come for a ride on my back?'

'I'm not sure about that,' said the monkey.

'I'm sure you'd enjoy it,' said the shark. 'You could hold on to my fin and we could swim through the waves as fast as you like. Think of the spray and the cool breeze in your fur. I could show you the wonderful place where the king of the sharks lives.'

The monkey climbed on the shark's back and they swam through the waves at a terrific pace. There was a broad grin on the shark's terrible jaws. 'What a foolish little animal you are,' said the shark, 'to have been tricked so easily. The king of the sharks is very ill. His doctors say that the only thing that will cure him is a monkey's heart. That's why we are going to see him. He's going to eat you.'

'Oh dear,' said the monkey. 'I wish you'd told me sooner. I haven't brought my heart with me. I've left it hanging in the cocoa tree. Your king will be very angry when he finds I have no heart. I'm sure he will punish you.'

'Oh no he won't,' snapped the shark. 'I wouldn't be so stupid as to take him a monkey with no heart. We'll just have to go back to the cocoa tree and get it.'

The shark swam back to the shore and the monkey jumped into the cocoa tree.

'Hurry up,' said the shark. 'We haven't got much time. I'll be in trouble if I'm late.'

'Hold on,' said the monkey, 'and I'll throw it down to you.' A pile of rotten fruit hit the shark on the nose. 'What a foolish shark you are to have been tricked so easily,' laughed the monkey.

The Stone Monkey

Long ago, when the world was fresh and new, the gods lived in palaces in the sky and looked after the people and animals living upon the Earth.

On top of one of Earth's mountains was a stone egg. Nobody knew where the egg had come from nor what might be inside it. One day the egg began to tremble and crack and out stepped a monkey. What was unusual about the monkey was that he was made of stone.

The stone monkey was very special in many ways. He was cleverer than other monkeys; he was much stronger than other monkeys; he was noisier than other monkeys; and he was also more mischievous. It is not surprising that he became king of the monkeys.

The stone monkey liked being king. He wanted to be the cleverest king that had ever lived. Every day he studied books of magic. He taught himself how to fly upon the clouds, to change himself into any animal he wanted, and to make himself invisible. You might think that he became a very wise monkey indeed. But you would be wrong. He liked mischief best of all and spent most of his time playing silly tricks on everyone. He also became very big-headed.

‘I’m bored with being king of the monkeys,’ said the stone monkey one day. ‘I should be king of all the animals that live on the Earth. In fact, I should be king of all the gods. I shall jump up to the heavens and make myself Lord of the Sky.’

The stone monkey flew to the sky palace and demanded to see Lord Buddha.

‘Hello, Monkey,’ said Lord Buddha. ‘What do you want?’

‘I want to be Lord of the Sky,’ laughed the stone monkey. ‘I’d make a much better job of it than you.’

‘Very well,’ said Lord Buddha, smiling. ‘All you have to do is pass one simple test. You must stand on my wrist and jump over my fingers.’

‘Is that all?’ laughed the stone monkey. ‘I can do far greater things than that.’

Lord Buddha stretched out his hand and the monkey got ready to make his jump. He took a deep breath and sprang into the sky. He jumped so high and flew so fast that he soon reached the very edge of the world. At the edge of the world stood five huge red pillars. Beyond the pillars there was nothing but empty space.

'Now I shall be Lord of the Sky,' laughed the stone monkey. 'Fancy thinking I couldn't jump out of his hand! I shall leave my mark on one of these pillars and bring Lord Buddha here to show him how far I can jump.' He wrote on one of the pillars, and with another giant leap flew back to the sky palace.

'When are you going to start your jump, Monkey?' smiled Lord Buddha.

'Start my jump! Start it!' shouted the stone monkey. 'I have been to the edge of the world and back. To prove it I wrote on one of the pillars I saw there. Come with me and I'll show you.'

'Do you mean *this* writing?' asked Lord Buddha, showing monkey his finger. On his finger was the mark the stone monkey had made. 'The whole world is in my hand,' said Lord Buddha. 'You could never have jumped out of it. You are a greedy monkey, who wants everything. Go back down to Earth, and learn to be happy with the things you have.'

The stone monkey was very ashamed of himself. He went back to Earth, to the kingdom of the monkeys, and ruled his subjects wisely and well.

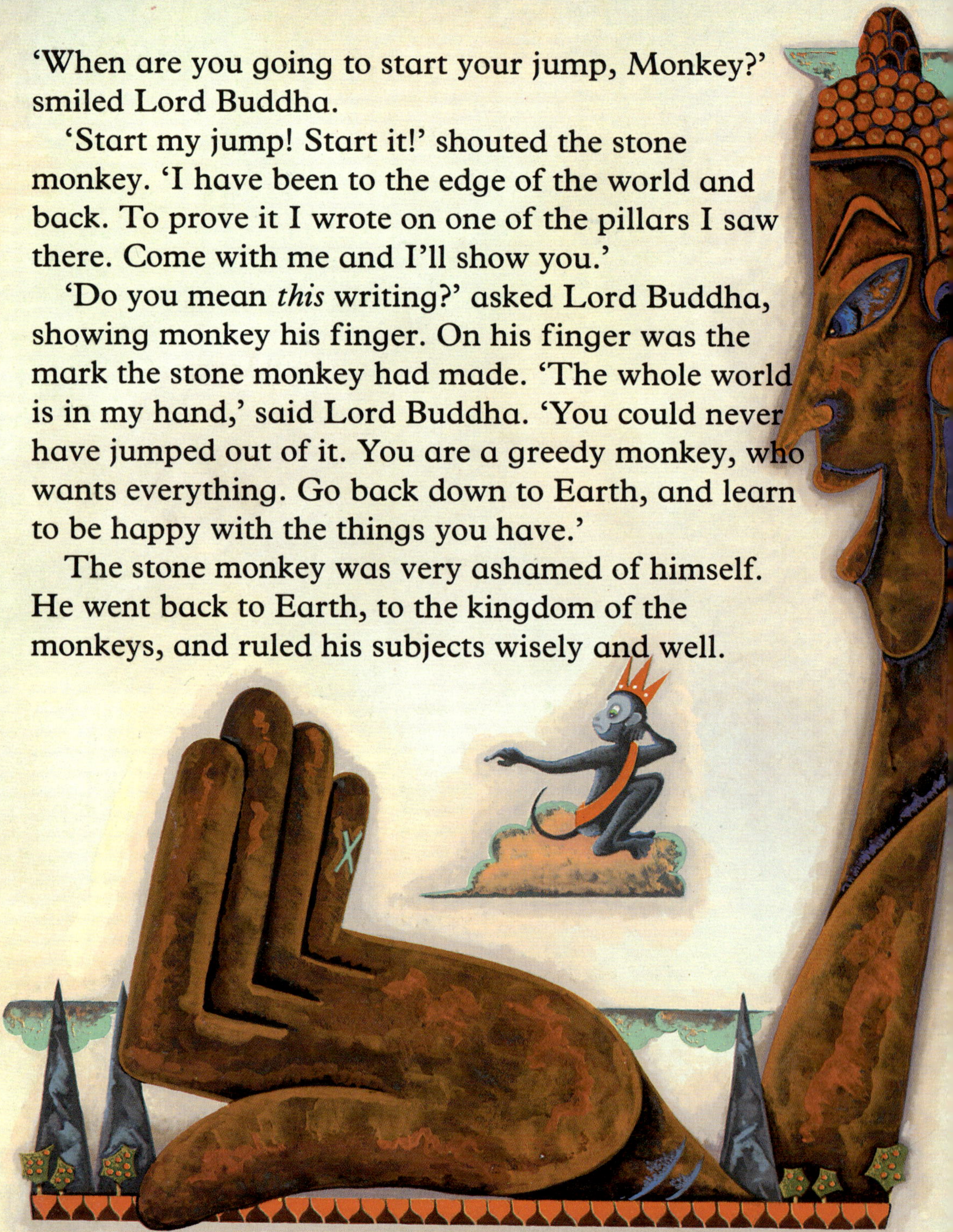